The
Write Method
Journal

LEGACY launch pad PUBLISHING

ISBN: 978-1-956955-30-9 (paperback)

978-1-956955-37-8 (hardcover)

978-1-956955-36-1 (ebook)

DISCLAIMER

The information contained in this journal is for informational purposes only. No material in here is intended to be a substitute for professional medical advice, diagnosis or treatment. Always seek the advice of your physician or other qualified health care provider with any questions you may have regarding a medical condition or treatment and before undertaking a new health care regimen, and never disregard professional medical advice or delay in seeking it because of something you have read in this journal.

FOR MORE INFORMATION, SCAN THIS CODE

FROM THE CREATORS…

A MESSAGE FROM ANNA DAVID

As a coach, I've worked with countless people on bettering their lives. As a writer, I've gazed at my navel, interviewed people both fascinating and not and articulated my feelings on paper perhaps more than anyone should.

I've also kept a journal since the age of six (when I graded my days and days when my mom took us to McDonald's got an automatic A+), which means I have stacks and stacks of books filled with scribbles that at the time I surely though betrayed undeniable genius and today would be horrified to have anyone read (including myself).

But I realized something at six that still holds true to this day: nothing provides more healing for me than writing out my feelings.

Still, many of the people I've worked with are stymied by that direction. "What should I write about?" I've heard more times than I can count.

Over time, in order to answer that question, I've taken the journaling prompts I've developed over the years, added 12-step elements and landed on a process that leaves me feeling… well, whole. Like my best self.

I've shared these prompts with the people I've worked with and witnessed incredible results: I've seen some overcome seemingly impossible circumstances, change their entire perspective and develop entirely new careers—and better lives.

I've watched others come up with business ideas and turn them into thriving enterprises and seen still others go from book idea to bestselling author. Yes, journaling can turn someone without direction into an entrepreneur or author (or both!) But, most important of all, it boosts happiness. Psychology Today (and countless other sources) have said that. And so does my experience—and the experiences of those I've worked with.

Because I know my limitations, I didn't want to publish this without some set of official confirmation that it was effective. And so I turned to the best medical source I know: Dr. Josh Lichtman, a prominent psychiatrist who is dual board-certified in adult psychiatry and addiction medicine.

In the end, we developed a journaling method that consists of nine daily questions that encompass nine essential elements. The elements are:

- Helping (Finding ways to be of service)
- Acknowledging (Addressing resentments)
- Progressing (Setting and working toward goals)
- Participating (Joining that day's flow of life)
- Identifying (Discovering and examining your fears)
- Nourishing (Taking care of yourself)
- Embracing (Giving up control)
- Seeking (Connecting with a Higher Power)
- Savoring (Uncovering gratitude)

You may notice something that has everything to do with item number six on the list: this list spells out HAPPINESS. We swear this wasn't intentional, which means it had to be noticing a coincidence—AKA faith. (As the saying goes, coincidences are the universe's way of staying anonymous.)

The reason happiness is the end result of following these prompts is that when we're paying attention to these things, we become who we are without our egos and natural human tendency toward negativity clouding our perception.

While this journal is meant to be completed in a month, do NOT let it become an albatross—another thing you could beat yourself up for not doing. If you miss a night, just pick it up the next night. Or a week later. Or a month later. Doing it even just once might change your perspective for good!

A MESSAGE FROM DR. JOSH LICHTMAN

I'M CERTAINLY NOT the first to note that we're living in a challenging time and I'm also not the first to point out the human tendency toward negativity.

None of us can control what's happening in the world today, not to mention what happens to us. The only thing we can control is how we react to it. And while medication and various forms of therapy can work wonders, there is a far simpler way to improve our mood.

That way is simply to pay attention to what's happening internally and to take note of when we're veering off track. A 2003 study out of UC Davis showed that people who kept gratitude journals on a weekly basis exercised more regularly, reported fewer physical symptoms, felt better about their lives as a whole and were more optimistic about the upcoming week compared to those who recorded hassles or neutral life events.

That's what makes The Write Method special.

It guides you through nine questions designed to make you take stock, feel grateful and get inspired. I promise you that practicing The Write Method is only going to make you want to practice it more.

We've included below some sample answers to the questions posed here. You can do much "bigger" or "smaller" acts than the ones listed; they're only meant to inspire anyone who's lost in the "I don't know what to write down" head space.

You have more control over how you feel than you may realize. Welcome to your new way of thinking, feeling and acting.

1

Today's Date _____

Who did I help today?

_____

_____

_____

Do I have any resentments I haven't dealt with? If I do have
resentments, what part do I play in them? How would a
Higher Power have me look at my resentment?

_____

_____

_____

_____

_____

_____

_____

_____

What goals did I work toward today?

_____

_____

_____

How did I join the flow of life today?

_____

_____

_____

Do I have any unexamined fears? If so, what is underneath the fear? How would a Higher Power have me look at my fear?

_____

_____

_____

_____

_____

_____

_____

_____

_____

_____

_____

_____

_____

_____

_____

How did I practice self-care today?

_____

_____

_____

How did I surrender control today?

_____

_____

_____

What signs can I see that a Higher Power is looking out for me?

_____

_____

_____

What are five things I'm grateful for right now?

_____

_____

_____

_____

_____

_____

_____

_____

_____

Today's Date _____

Who did I help today?

_____

_____

_____

Do I have any resentments I haven't dealt with? If I do have
resentments, what part do I play in them? How would a
Higher Power have me look at my resentment?

_____

_____

_____

_____

_____

_____

_____

_____

What goals did I work toward today?

_____

_____

_____

How did I join the flow of life today?

_____

_____

_____

Do I have any unexamined fears? If so, what is underneath the fear? How would a Higher Power have me look at my fear?

_____

_____

_____

_____

_____

_____

_____

_____

_____

_____

_____

_____

_____

How did I practice self-care today?

_____

_____

_____

How did I surrender control today?

_____

_____

_____

What signs can I see that a Higher Power is looking out for me?

_____

_____

_____

What are five things I'm grateful for right now?

_____

_____

_____

_____

_____

_____

_____

_____

Today's Date _____

Who did I help today?

_____

_____

_____

Do I have any resentments I haven't dealt with? If I do have resentments, what part do I play in them? How would a Higher Power have me look at my resentment?

_____

_____

_____

_____

_____

_____

_____

_____

What goals did I work toward today?

_____

_____

_____

How did I join the flow of life today?

_____

_____

_____

Do I have any unexamined fears? If so, what is underneath the fear? How would a Higher Power have me look at my fear?

_____

_____

_____

_____

_____

_____

_____

_____

_____

_____

_____

_____

_____

_____

How did I practice self-care today?

_____

_____

_____

How did I surrender control today?

_____

_____

_____

What signs can I see that a Higher Power is looking out for me?

_____

_____

_____

What are five things I'm grateful for right now?

_____

_____

_____

_____

_____

_____

_____

_____

_____

_____

Today's Date _____

Who did I help today?

_____

_____

_____

Do I have any resentments I haven't dealt with? If I do have resentments, what part do I play in them? How would a Higher Power have me look at my resentment?

_____

_____

_____

_____

_____

_____

_____

_____

What goals did I work toward today?

_____

_____

_____

How did I join the flow of life today?

_____

_____

_____

Do I have any unexamined fears? If so, what is underneath the fear? How would a Higher Power have me look at my fear?

_____

_____

_____

_____

_____

_____

_____

_____

_____

_____

_____

_____

_____

How did I practice self-care today?

_____

_____

_____

How did I surrender control today?

_____

_____

_____

What signs can I see that a Higher Power is looking out for me?

_____

_____

_____

What are five things I'm grateful for right now?

_____

_____

_____

_____

_____

_____

_____

_____

_____

Today's Date _____

Who did I help today?

_____

_____

_____

Do I have any resentments I haven't dealt with? If I do have
resentments, what part do I play in them? How would a
Higher Power have me look at my resentment?

_____

_____

_____

_____

_____

_____

_____

_____

What goals did I work toward today?

_____

_____

_____

How did I join the flow of life today?

_____

_____

_____

Do I have any unexamined fears? If so, what is underneath the fear? How would a Higher Power have me look at my fear?

_____

_____

_____

_____

_____

_____

_____

_____

_____

_____

_____

_____

_____

_____

How did I practice self-care today?

_____

_____

_____

How did I surrender control today?

_____

_____

_____

What signs can I see that a Higher Power is looking out for me?

_____

_____

_____

What are five things I'm grateful for right now?

_____

_____

_____

_____

_____

_____

_____

_____

_____

6

Today's Date _____

Who did I help today?

_____

_____

_____

Do I have any resentments I haven't dealt with? If I do have resentments, what part do I play in them? How would a Higher Power have me look at my resentment?

_____

_____

_____

_____

_____

_____

_____

_____

What goals did I work toward today?

_____

_____

_____

How did I join the flow of life today?

_____

_____

_____

Do I have any unexamined fears? If so, what is underneath the fear? How would a Higher Power have me look at my fear?

_____

_____

_____

_____

_____

_____

_____

_____

_____

_____

_____

_____

_____

How did I practice self-care today?

_____
_____
_____

How did I surrender control today?

_____
_____
_____

What signs can I see that a Higher Power is looking out for me?

_____
_____
_____

What are five things I'm grateful for right now?

_____
_____
_____
_____
_____
_____
_____
_____
_____

Today's Date _____

Who did I help today?

_____

_____

_____

Do I have any resentments I haven't dealt with? If I do have
resentments, what part do I play in them? How would a
Higher Power have me look at my resentment?

_____

_____

_____

_____

_____

_____

_____

What goals did I work toward today?

_____

_____

_____

How did I join the flow of life today?

_____

_____

_____

Do I have any unexamined fears? If so, what is underneath the fear? How would a Higher Power have me look at my fear?

_____

_____

_____

_____

_____

_____

_____

_____

_____

_____

_____

_____

_____

How did I practice self-care today?

_____

_____

_____

How did I surrender control today?

_____

_____

_____

What signs can I see that a Higher Power is looking out for me?

_____

_____

_____

What are five things I'm grateful for right now?

_____

_____

_____

_____

_____

_____

_____

_____

_____

8

Today's Date _____

Who did I help today?

_____

_____

_____

Do I have any resentments I haven't dealt with? If I do have
resentments, what part do I play in them? How would a
Higher Power have me look at my resentment?

_____

_____

_____

_____

_____

_____

_____

_____

What goals did I work toward today?

_____

_____

_____

How did I join the flow of life today?

_____

_____

_____

Do I have any unexamined fears? If so, what is underneath the fear? How would a Higher Power have me look at my fear?

_____

_____

_____

_____

_____

_____

_____

_____

_____

_____

_____

_____

_____

How did I practice self-care today?

_____

_____

_____

How did I surrender control today?

_____

_____

_____

What signs can I see that a Higher Power is looking out for me?

_____

_____

_____

What are five things I'm grateful for right now?

_____

_____

_____

_____

_____

_____

_____

_____

_____

9

Today's Date _____

Who did I help today?

_____
_____
_____

Do I have any resentments I haven't dealt with? If I do have resentments, what part do I play in them? How would a Higher Power have me look at my resentment?

_____
_____
_____
_____
_____
_____
_____
_____

What goals did I work toward today?

_____

_____

_____

How did I join the flow of life today?

_____

_____

_____

Do I have any unexamined fears? If so, what is underneath the fear? How would a Higher Power have me look at my fear?

_____

_____

_____

_____

_____

_____

_____

_____

_____

_____

_____

_____

_____

_____

How did I practice self-care today?

_____

_____

_____

How did I surrender control today?

_____

_____

_____

What signs can I see that a Higher Power is looking out for me?

_____

_____

_____

What are five things I'm grateful for right now?

_____

_____

_____

_____

_____

_____

_____

_____

_____

Today's Date _____

Who did I help today?

_____

_____

_____

Do I have any resentments I haven't dealt with? If I do have resentments, what part do I play in them? How would a Higher Power have me look at my resentment?

_____

_____

_____

_____

_____

_____

_____

_____

What goals did I work toward today?

_____

_____

_____

How did I join the flow of life today?

_____

_____

_____

Do I have any unexamined fears? If so, what is underneath the fear? How would a Higher Power have me look at my fear?

_____

_____

_____

_____

_____

_____

_____

_____

_____

_____

_____

_____

_____

How did I practice self-care today?

_____

_____

_____

How did I surrender control today?

_____

_____

_____

What signs can I see that a Higher Power is looking out for me?

_____

_____

_____

What are five things I'm grateful for right now?

_____

_____

_____

_____

_____

_____

_____

_____

_____

Today's Date _____

Who did I help today?

_____

_____

_____

Do I have any resentments I haven't dealt with? If I do have resentments, what part do I play in them? How would a Higher Power have me look at my resentment?

_____

_____

_____

_____

_____

_____

_____

_____

What goals did I work toward today?

_____

_____

_____

How did I join the flow of life today?

_____

_____

_____

Do I have any unexamined fears? If so, what is underneath the fear? How would a Higher Power have me look at my fear?

_____

_____

_____

_____

_____

_____

_____

_____

_____

_____

_____

_____

_____

How did I practice self-care today?

_____

_____

_____

How did I surrender control today?

_____

_____

_____

What signs can I see that a Higher Power is looking out for me?

_____

_____

_____

What are five things I'm grateful for right now?

_____

_____

_____

_____

_____

_____

_____

_____

Today's Date _____

Who did I help today?

_____

_____

_____

Do I have any resentments I haven't dealt with? If I do have resentments, what part do I play in them? How would a Higher Power have me look at my resentment?

_____

_____

_____

_____

_____

_____

_____

_____

What goals did I work toward today?

_____

_____

_____

How did I join the flow of life today?

_____

_____

_____

Do I have any unexamined fears? If so, what is underneath the fear? How would a Higher Power have me look at my fear?

_____

_____

_____

_____

_____

_____

_____

_____

_____

_____

_____

_____

_____

How did I practice self-care today?

_____

_____

_____

How did I surrender control today?

_____

_____

_____

What signs can I see that a Higher Power is looking out for me?

_____

_____

_____

What are five things I'm grateful for right now?

_____

_____

_____

_____

_____

_____

_____

_____

_____

_____

Today's Date _____

Who did I help today?

_____

_____

_____

Do I have any resentments I haven't dealt with? If I do have resentments, what part do I play in them? How would a Higher Power have me look at my resentment?

_____

_____

_____

_____

_____

_____

_____

_____

What goals did I work toward today?

_____

_____

_____

How did I join the flow of life today?

_____

_____

_____

Do I have any unexamined fears? If so, what is underneath the fear? How would a Higher Power have me look at my fear?

_____

_____

_____

_____

_____

_____

_____

_____

_____

_____

_____

_____

How did I practice self-care today?

_____

_____

_____

How did I surrender control today?

_____

_____

_____

What signs can I see that a Higher Power is looking out for me?

_____

_____

_____

What are five things I'm grateful for right now?

_____

_____

_____

_____

_____

_____

_____

_____

_____

_____

Today's Date _____

Who did I help today?

_____
_____
_____

Do I have any resentments I haven't dealt with? If I do have resentments, what part do I play in them? How would a Higher Power have me look at my resentment?

_____
_____
_____
_____
_____
_____
_____
_____

What goals did I work toward today?

_____

_____

_____

How did I join the flow of life today?

_____

_____

_____

Do I have any unexamined fears? If so, what is underneath the fear? How would a Higher Power have me look at my fear?

_____

_____

_____

_____

_____

_____

_____

_____

_____

_____

_____

_____

_____

_____

How did I practice self-care today?

_____

_____

_____

How did I surrender control today?

_____

_____

_____

What signs can I see that a Higher Power is looking out for me?

_____

_____

_____

What are five things I'm grateful for right now?

_____

_____

_____

_____

_____

_____

_____

_____

_____

Today's Date _____

Who did I help today?

_____

_____

_____

Do I have any resentments I haven't dealt with? If I do have resentments, what part do I play in them? How would a Higher Power have me look at my resentment?

_____

_____

_____

_____

_____

_____

_____

_____

What goals did I work toward today?

_____

_____

_____

How did I join the flow of life today?

_____

_____

_____

Do I have any unexamined fears? If so, what is underneath the fear? How would a Higher Power have me look at my fear?

_____

_____

_____

_____

_____

_____

_____

_____

_____

_____

_____

_____

_____

How did I practice self-care today?

_____

_____

_____

How did I surrender control today?

_____

_____

_____

What signs can I see that a Higher Power is looking out for me?

_____

_____

_____

What are five things I'm grateful for right now?

_____

_____

_____

_____

_____

_____

_____

_____

_____

Today's Date _____

Who did I help today?

_____

_____

_____

Do I have any resentments I haven't dealt with? If I do have resentments, what part do I play in them? How would a Higher Power have me look at my resentment?

_____

_____

_____

_____

_____

_____

_____

_____

What goals did I work toward today?

_____

_____

_____

How did I join the flow of life today?

_____

_____

_____

Do I have any unexamined fears? If so, what is underneath the fear? How would a Higher Power have me look at my fear?

_____

_____

_____

_____

_____

_____

_____

_____

_____

_____

_____

_____

_____

How did I practice self-care today?

_____

_____

_____

How did I surrender control today?

_____

_____

_____

What signs can I see that a Higher Power is looking out for me?

_____

_____

_____

What are five things I'm grateful for right now?

_____

_____

_____

_____

_____

_____

_____

_____

_____

17

Today's Date _____

Who did I help today?

_____

_____

_____

Do I have any resentments I haven't dealt with? If I do have
resentments, what part do I play in them? How would a
Higher Power have me look at my resentment?

_____

_____

_____

_____

_____

_____

_____

_____

What goals did I work toward today?

_____

_____

_____

How did I join the flow of life today?

_____

_____

_____

Do I have any unexamined fears? If so, what is underneath the fear? How would a Higher Power have me look at my fear?

_____

_____

_____

_____

_____

_____

_____

_____

_____

_____

_____

_____

_____

How did I practice self-care today?

_____

_____

_____

How did I surrender control today?

_____

_____

_____

What signs can I see that a Higher Power is looking out for me?

_____

_____

_____

What are five things I'm grateful for right now?

_____

_____

_____

_____

_____

_____

_____

_____

_____

Today's Date _____

Who did I help today?

_____

_____

_____

Do I have any resentments I haven't dealt with? If I do have resentments, what part do I play in them? How would a Higher Power have me look at my resentment?

_____

_____

_____

_____

_____

_____

_____

What goals did I work toward today?

_____

_____

_____

How did I join the flow of life today?

_____

_____

_____

Do I have any unexamined fears? If so, what is underneath the fear? How would a Higher Power have me look at my fear?

_____

_____

_____

_____

_____

_____

_____

_____

_____

_____

_____

_____

_____

How did I practice self-care today?

_____

_____

_____

How did I surrender control today?

_____

_____

_____

What signs can I see that a Higher Power is looking out for me?

_____

_____

_____

What are five things I'm grateful for right now?

_____

_____

_____

_____

_____

_____

_____

_____

_____

19

Today's Date _____

Who did I help today?

_____
_____
_____

Do I have any resentments I haven't dealt with? If I do have
resentments, what part do I play in them? How would a
Higher Power have me look at my resentment?

_____
_____
_____
_____
_____
_____
_____
_____

What goals did I work toward today?

_____

_____

_____

How did I join the flow of life today?

_____

_____

_____

Do I have any unexamined fears? If so, what is underneath the fear? How would a Higher Power have me look at my fear?

_____

_____

_____

_____

_____

_____

_____

_____

_____

_____

_____

_____

_____

_____

How did I practice self-care today?

_____

_____

_____

How did I surrender control today?

_____

_____

_____

What signs can I see that a Higher Power is looking out for me?

_____

_____

_____

What are five things I'm grateful for right now?

_____

_____

_____

_____

_____

_____

_____

_____

_____

Today's Date _____

Who did I help today?

_____

_____

_____

Do I have any resentments I haven't dealt with? If I do have resentments, what part do I play in them? How would a Higher Power have me look at my resentment?

_____

_____

_____

_____

_____

_____

_____

_____

What goals did I work toward today?

_____

_____

_____

How did I join the flow of life today?

_____

_____

_____

Do I have any unexamined fears? If so, what is underneath the fear? How would a Higher Power have me look at my fear?

_____

_____

_____

_____

_____

_____

_____

_____

_____

_____

_____

_____

_____

How did I practice self-care today?

_____

_____

_____

How did I surrender control today?

_____

_____

_____

What signs can I see that a Higher Power is looking out for me?

_____

_____

_____

What are five things I'm grateful for right now?

_____

_____

_____

_____

_____

_____

_____

_____

_____

Today's Date _____

Who did I help today?

_____

_____

_____

Do I have any resentments I haven't dealt with? If I do have resentments, what part do I play in them? How would a Higher Power have me look at my resentment?

_____

_____

_____

_____

_____

_____

_____

_____

What goals did I work toward today?

_____

_____

_____

How did I join the flow of life today?

_____

_____

_____

Do I have any unexamined fears? If so, what is underneath the fear? How would a Higher Power have me look at my fear?

_____

_____

_____

_____

_____

_____

_____

_____

_____

_____

_____

_____

_____

_____

How did I practice self-care today?

_____

_____

_____

How did I surrender control today?

_____

_____

_____

What signs can I see that a Higher Power is looking out for me?

_____

_____

_____

What are five things I'm grateful for right now?

_____

_____

_____

_____

_____

_____

_____

_____

_____

Today's Date _____

Who did I help today?

_____

_____

_____

Do I have any resentments I haven't dealt with? If I do have resentments, what part do I play in them? How would a Higher Power have me look at my resentment?

_____

_____

_____

_____

_____

_____

_____

_____

What goals did I work toward today?

_____

_____

_____

How did I join the flow of life today?

_____

_____

_____

Do I have any unexamined fears? If so, what is underneath the fear? How would a Higher Power have me look at my fear?

_____

_____

_____

_____

_____

_____

_____

_____

_____

_____

_____

_____

_____

How did I practice self-care today?

_____

_____

_____

How did I surrender control today?

_____

_____

_____

What signs can I see that a Higher Power is looking out for me?

_____

_____

_____

What are five things I'm grateful for right now?

_____

_____

_____

_____

_____

_____

_____

_____

_____

Today's Date _____

Who did I help today?

_____

_____

_____

Do I have any resentments I haven't dealt with? If I do have
resentments, what part do I play in them? How would a
Higher Power have me look at my resentment?

_____

_____

_____

_____

_____

_____

_____

_____

What goals did I work toward today?

_____

_____

_____

How did I join the flow of life today?

_____

_____

_____

Do I have any unexamined fears? If so, what is underneath the
fear? How would a Higher Power have me look at my fear?

_____

_____

_____

_____

_____

_____

_____

_____

_____

_____

_____

_____

_____

How did I practice self-care today?

_____

_____

_____

How did I surrender control today?

_____

_____

_____

What signs can I see that a Higher Power is looking out for me?

_____

_____

_____

What are five things I'm grateful for right now?

_____

_____

_____

_____

_____

_____

_____

_____

Today's Date _____

Who did I help today?

_____

_____

_____

Do I have any resentments I haven't dealt with? If I do have resentments, what part do I play in them? How would a Higher Power have me look at my resentment?

_____

_____

_____

_____

_____

_____

_____

_____

What goals did I work toward today?

_____

_____

_____

How did I join the flow of life today?

_____

_____

_____

Do I have any unexamined fears? If so, what is underneath the fear? How would a Higher Power have me look at my fear?

_____

_____

_____

_____

_____

_____

_____

_____

_____

_____

_____

_____

_____

_____

How did I practice self-care today?

_____

_____

_____

How did I surrender control today?

_____

_____

_____

What signs can I see that a Higher Power is looking out for me?

_____

_____

_____

What are five things I'm grateful for right now?

_____

_____

_____

_____

_____

_____

_____

_____

_____

_____

Today's Date _____

Who did I help today?

_____

_____

_____

Do I have any resentments I haven't dealt with? If I do have
resentments, what part do I play in them? How would a
Higher Power have me look at my resentment?

_____

_____

_____

_____

_____

_____

_____

_____

What goals did I work toward today?

_____

_____

_____

How did I join the flow of life today?

_____

_____

_____

Do I have any unexamined fears? If so, what is underneath the fear? How would a Higher Power have me look at my fear?

_____

_____

_____

_____

_____

_____

_____

_____

_____

_____

_____

_____

_____

How did I practice self-care today?

_____

_____

_____

How did I surrender control today?

_____

_____

_____

What signs can I see that a Higher Power is looking out for
me?

_____

_____

_____

What are five things I'm grateful for right now?

_____

_____

_____

_____

_____

_____

_____

_____

Today's Date _____

Who did I help today?

_____

_____

_____

Do I have any resentments I haven't dealt with? If I do have resentments, what part do I play in them? How would a Higher Power have me look at my resentment?

_____

_____

_____

_____

_____

_____

_____

_____

What goals did I work toward today?

_____

_____

_____

How did I join the flow of life today?

_____

_____

_____

Do I have any unexamined fears? If so, what is underneath the
fear? How would a Higher Power have me look at my fear?

_____

_____

_____

_____

_____

_____

_____

_____

_____

_____

_____

_____

_____

How did I practice self-care today?

_____

_____

_____

How did I surrender control today?

_____

_____

_____

What signs can I see that a Higher Power is looking out for me?

_____

_____

_____

What are five things I'm grateful for right now?

_____

_____

_____

_____

_____

_____

_____

_____

_____

Today's Date _____

Who did I help today?

_____

_____

_____

Do I have any resentments I haven't dealt with? If I do have
resentments, what part do I play in them? How would a
Higher Power have me look at my resentment?

_____

_____

_____

_____

_____

_____

_____

_____

What goals did I work toward today?

_____

_____

_____

How did I join the flow of life today?

_____

_____

_____

Do I have any unexamined fears? If so, what is underneath the fear? How would a Higher Power have me look at my fear?

_____

_____

_____

_____

_____

_____

_____

_____

_____

_____

_____

_____

_____

_____

How did I practice self-care today?

_____

_____

_____

How did I surrender control today?

_____

_____

_____

What signs can I see that a Higher Power is looking out for me?

_____

_____

_____

What are five things I'm grateful for right now?

_____

_____

_____

_____

_____

_____

_____

_____

_____

_____

Today's Date _____

Who did I help today?

_____
_____
_____

Do I have any resentments I haven't dealt with? If I do have resentments, what part do I play in them? How would a Higher Power have me look at my resentment?

_____
_____
_____
_____
_____
_____
_____
_____

What goals did I work toward today?

_____

_____

_____

How did I join the flow of life today?

_____

_____

_____

Do I have any unexamined fears? If so, what is underneath the fear? How would a Higher Power have me look at my fear?

_____

_____

_____

_____

_____

_____

_____

_____

_____

_____

_____

_____

_____

How did I practice self-care today?

_____

_____

_____

How did I surrender control today?

_____

_____

_____

What signs can I see that a Higher Power is looking out for me?

_____

_____

_____

What are five things I'm grateful for right now?

_____

_____

_____

_____

_____

_____

_____

_____

_____

_____

Today's Date _____

Who did I help today?

_____

_____

_____

Do I have any resentments I haven't dealt with? If I do have
resentments, what part do I play in them? How would a
Higher Power have me look at my resentment?

_____

_____

_____

_____

_____

_____

_____

_____

What goals did I work toward today?

_____

_____

_____

How did I join the flow of life today?

_____

_____

_____

Do I have any unexamined fears? If so, what is underneath the fear? How would a Higher Power have me look at my fear?

_____

_____

_____

_____

_____

_____

_____

_____

_____

_____

_____

_____

_____

How did I practice self-care today?

_____

_____

_____

How did I surrender control today?

_____

_____

_____

What signs can I see that a Higher Power is looking out for me?

_____

_____

_____

What are five things I'm grateful for right now?

_____

_____

_____

_____

_____

_____

_____

_____

_____

Today's Date _____

Who did I help today?

_____

_____

_____

Do I have any resentments I haven't dealt with? If I do have
resentments, what part do I play in them? How would a
Higher Power have me look at my resentment?

_____

_____

_____

_____

_____

_____

_____

_____

What goals did I work toward today?

_____

_____

_____

How did I join the flow of life today?

_____

_____

_____

Do I have any unexamined fears? If so, what is underneath the
fear? How would a Higher Power have me look at my fear?

_____

_____

_____

_____

_____

_____

_____

_____

_____

_____

_____

_____

_____

How did I practice self-care today?

_____

_____

_____

How did I surrender control today?

_____

_____

_____

What signs can I see that a Higher Power is looking out for me?

_____

_____

_____

What are five things I'm grateful for right now?

_____

_____

_____

_____

_____

_____

_____

_____

ABOUT THE CREATORS

Anna David is a *New York Times* bestselling author of eight books, founder of Legacy Launch Pad Publishing and three-time TEDx speaker who has appeared on *Good Morning America, Today Show, The Talk* and dozens of other programs. Her first novel, *Party Girl*, is in development as a feature film. She's the on-air book critic for KATU Portland and hosts the hit podcast Entrepreneur Publishing Academy. Sober for over two decades, Anna coaches both writers and addicts in recovery.

Dr. Josh Lichtman has been practicing psychiatry for almost two decades. He is dual board certified in both adult psychiatry and addiction medicine.

He is passionate about mindfulness practice and psychiatry and is constantly trying to blend the two. Although he primarily focuses on TMS and psychopharmacology, he is trained in various modalities of psychotherapy including CBT, DBT, EMDR and Psychodynamic Psychotherapy. He is a clinical instructor at UCLA, and has been selected to be on the list for Southern California Super Doctors for 2021, 2020, 2019, 2018, 2017, 2016 and 2015.

FOR MORE INFORMATION, SCAN
THIS CODE